BOOTCAMP BEAUTIES

WAG BOOKS

INTRODUCTION

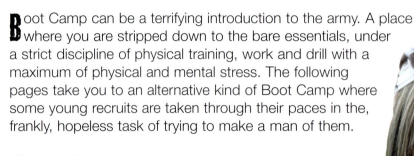

Boot Camp can be a terrifying introduction to the army. A place where you are stripped down to the bare essentials, under a strict discipline of physical training, work and drill with a maximum of physical and mental stress. The following pages take you to an alternative kind of Boot Camp where some young recruits are taken through their paces in the, frankly, hopeless task of trying to make a man of them.

Although these young ladies showed enthusiasm and a willingness to learn how to handle the tools of their trade their instructor had more than a little trouble in getting them down in the dirt. However, they all had a couple of strong points. They proved to be very good in the rear and liked any form of standing to attention, especially when helmets were involved. Whether these raw recruits would make an enemy run for their lives is debatable.

Boot Camp is renowned for its regimen of physical exercise, and these recruits showed they couldn't get enough of it. Their training involved the usual round of physical jerks and squat thrusts: they humped loads, they climbed greasy poles and they wrestled with snakes. "Drop and give me twenty!" was the cry from many a staff sergeant, baton in hand. While many recruits wanted to buck the system and kick against the pricks, they all had to pay lip service to their superiors in the end.

And, as the final parade dawned, Boot Camp could be seen to have worked its magic. The recruits entered its gates inexperienced, they lost their innocence in Boot Camp, learned to handle weapons, and left behind a team of hardened instructors, who stood ramrod stiff and straight to a man to salute them as they left.

WAG books is an imprint of
Compendium Publishing
43 Frith Street, Soho,
London, W1D 4SA

Designed by Tony Stocks
Compendium Design
and Production

© Compendium Publishing 2004

All rights reserved. No part of this
publication may be reproduced or
transmitted in any form by any
means electronic or mechanical,
including photocopy, recording, or
in any information storage
and retrieval system,
without the prior permission of
the publishers.

A CIP catalogue record for
this book is available from
the British Library

ISBN 1 902579 83 6

Printed in Hong Kong through Printworks Int.Ltd.